HYPOCRISY IN RELIGION
A STUDY IN AMOS

BIBLE STUDIES TO IMPACT THE LIVES OF ORDINARY PEOPLE

Christian Focus Publications
The Word Worldwide

by Marie Dinnen

PREFACE

Where there's LIFE there's GROWTH:
Where there's GROWTH there's LIFE.

WHY GROW a study group?

Because as we study the Bible and share together we can

- learn to combat loneliness, depression, staleness, frustration, and other problems
- get to understand and love each other
- become responsive to the Holy Spirit's dealing and obedient to God's Word

and that's GROWTH.

How do you GROW a study group?

- Just start by asking a friend to join you and then aim at expanding your group.
- Study the set portions daily (they are brief and easy: no catches).
- Meet once a week to discuss what you find.
- Befriend others, both Christians and non Christians, and work away together

see how it GROWS!

WHEN you GROW ...

This will happen at school, at home, at work, at play, in your youth group, your student fellowship, women's meetings, mid-week meetings, churches and communities,

you'll be REACHING THROUGH TEACHING

AMOS • PREFACE

INTRODUCTORY STUDY

It's always a bit difficult to start digging into an Old Testament book, but as we search and share together we will find that the message of Amos has something for us today.

His Times
Bible Students assess the time of this book to around 760 BC. This would have been during the reign of Jeroboam II of Israel, a very prosperous period in the life of Israel. The Kingdom extended its borders until it was as extensive as in the days of Solomon, and Amos 6:13 seems to indicate that Jeroboam was very proud of his nation and military advance. Israel's control of the trade routes made her so prosperous that the wealthy class lived in great luxury, but with little regard for the privations of the lower and poorer class (2:12, 15; 5:11; 6:6). Humanly speaking, it looked as if Israel was made, but they had left God out of their reckoning (5:18 and 6:3).

His God
Amos, like Paul (I Cor. 8:5-6) believed in the One true God and rebuked Israel for taking heathen gods (5:26-27). Over and over again he uses terms for God which show Him as the Sovereign Lord, the Omnipotent One (4:13), the Moral Governor of all nations (2:16), etc.

His People
They were called the people of God and were privileged to know God's Word. Yet, they committed crimes against their fellow men and sinned against God despite their enlightenment (1:3; 2:4). Their crimes against men and sins against God showed clearly that their religion didn't mean anything really.

His Message
Although he warned Israel of pending judgment he prays that God will not write them off (7:2) and brings them hope and the promise of salvation (9:15).

His Qualifications
It is very clear that Amos did not profess to be a 'professional' prophet, but rather asserted that he was a very humble man through whom God chose to speak (7:14).

At the very time of preparing these notes I read in the daily newspaper:

'Canberra lower class are more prone to mental illness ...' The article following stated how wide was the gap between the well-educated, affluent society of Canberra, Australia's capital, and lower paid, unskilled workers. The concluding sentences of the article stated: 'It is inevitable that such people will be subjected to stresses which the more affluent, high status person can avoid. Social, recreational and cultural facilities are geared to the higher income inhabitants, and the less well-off have little contact with others of their own group.'

'The fact that a city has a high average level of affluence should not be allowed to hide the plight of the non affluent.'

In fact this study suggests that a high general level of affluence creates considerable problems for the minority not sharing this affluence.

It so happens that the newspaper report was on Canberra, but we know that there are many more situations throughout the world with similar and far more acute problems and even wider gaps than exist in Canberra.

So we see that the situation in which Amos lived wasn't peculiar to his times. It has been true in every generation and always will be true until the world finds the answer in the teaching of the Word of God.

Try to memorise the text highlighted at the end of each study.

STUDY 1

ALL ABOUT AMOS

QUESTIONS

DAY 1 *Amos 1:1-2.*
a) What brief description does Amos give about himself?
b) What had he seen and heard?

DAY 2 *Amos 1:1-2; 2 Kings 14:23-29.*
a) How does the 'Kings' reference suggest that Israel under Jeroboam was enjoying a period of prosperity?
b) What kind of moral and religious influence would Jeroboam have exercised on the nation?

DAY 3 *Amos 7:14.*
a) What was Amos' subsidiary occupation?
b) How would Amos' occupations have brought him in contact with the Northern Kingdom?

DAY 4 *Amos 7:14-15.*
a) What constituted Amos' call to the office of a prophet?
b) Had he been trained as a prophet?

DAY 5 *Amos 2:6-8; 4:4-5; 5:21.*
a) Could Israel have been described as 'religious'?
b) What was the moral fabric of the nation like?

DAY 6 *Hosea 1:1; 4:16-19; 5:3-5; 10:5-11.*
Hosea was a contemporary of Amos prophesying in the Southern Kingdom of Judah. How did he describe Israel?

DAY 7 *Amos 7:10-12; 9:11-15.*
Use these verses to summarise the message Amos was to proclaim.

MEMORY VERSE: Amos 1:3a

God often chooses someone from a humble background when He wants a job done. Moses could have lived on in Pharaoh's palace but God trained and prepared him in the desert to be Israel's leader (Exod. 3:1). David, a shepherd boy, was chosen to be king (I Sam. 16:11-13). Jesus, moulded in a carpenter's shop, became King of Kings (Matt. 13:55; 2 Cor. 8:9). The disciples were mainly a bunch of nobodies (Matt. 4:18-22; Luke 10:23-24).

> Thou did'st leave Thy throne and Thy Kingly crown
> When Thou camest to earth for me,
> But in Bethlehem's home was there found no room for Thy holy nativity.
> The foxes found rest and the birds a nest
> In the shade of the forest tree,
> But Thy couch was the sod, O Thou Son of God, in the deserts of Galilee.

So, inconspicuous Amos was chosen from a humble background. He was a simple shepherd and apparently augmented his income by cultivating and selling wild figs. Probably he went north to sell his wares in the more prosperous section of the country and saw there the sharp contrast between the upper and lower classes. In I Corinthians 1:27 we read that 'God has deliberately chosen to use ideas the world considers foolish and of little worth in order to shame those people considered by the world as wise and great' (LB).

In looking at Amos' life we can learn much of Christian character. He obviously had a sense of call (7:14-15). His message was from God, so he must have walked close to God (7:16-17). He had courage and would not compromise, despite powerful threats (7:10-17). His preaching was so simple and clear that men got its meaning and responded (7:12-13). His faith never wavered (9:11-15).

If you look up Matthew 10:24; Luke 14:26, 27, 33; 2 Corinthians 6:10; James 2:5, you will see that God has much to say to us about discipleship today.

To a shepherd, the roar of a lion means it is about to pounce on its prey. Amos proclaimed that God was about to descend in judgment and that Israel would be as helpless in God's hands as a lamb in the clutch of a lion. He foretold that famine would come, even to the very fertile region of Carmel.

Maybe we should consider at this stage whether we, too, can be hypocritical in our faith and forgetful of God. There is much in the Bible to warn us that spiritual famine is possible in our lives. Look up Psalm 106:15. Are we more concerned about getting our own way than letting the Lord have His way in our lives?

Thy way, not mine O Lord, however dark it be!
Lead me by Thine own hand, choose out the path for me.
I dare not choose my lot, I would not if I might,
Choose Thou for me, my God, so shall I walk aright.
Not mine, not mine the choice in things both great or small,
Be Thou my Guide, my Strength, my Wisdom and my All.

STUDY 2
EIGHT NATIONS AND THEIR SINS

QUESTIONS

(The recurring expression, 'For three sins ... even for four ...', is probably an idiom meaning 'For many sins'.)

DAY 1 *Amos 1:3-5.*
a) Why might denouncing foreign nations have attracted a crowd around Amos?
b) Why was Damascus (capital of Syria) to be judged? What insight does 2 Kings 8:12; 13:3, 4, 7 give into Syria's behaviour towards Israel?
c) How was this prophecy fulfilled (2 Kings 16:7-9)?

DAY 2 *Amos 1:6-10.*
a) Why were the Philistines and Phoenicia (Tyre) to be judged?
b) What treaty had probably been disregarded by Tyre (I Kings 5:1-12)?

DAY 3 *Amos 1:11-12; Psalm 137:7.*
a) What was the sin of Edom?
b) How does Edom's attitude contrast with that of God's (Isa. 57:15; Mic. 7:18-19)?
c) What advice does Ephesians 4:26 give us about anger?

DAY 4 *Amos 1:13-15.*
a) What was the root cause of Ammon's sin?
b) What are we warned about in I Timothy 6:6-11?

DAY 5 *Amos 2:1-3.*
a) What 'small' thing had God noticed about Moab? What is underlined in Proverbs 15:3; Hebrews 4:13?
b) What reasons are assigned for Moab's downfall in Jeremiah 48:1, 7, 29, 30, 42?

DAY 6 *Amos 2:4-5.*
a) What specific charges are laid against Judah?
b) What is the best way to respond to God's Word (Jas. 1:22-25)?

QUESTIONS (contd.)

DAY 7 *Amos 2:6-8.*
a) Why would Amos' audience now begin to feel uncomfortable?
b) What list of sins was Israel charged with?

MEMORY VERSE: Amos 2:4

Syria in general and *Damascus* in particular were to be judged because of cruelty. They are reputed to have mutilated their enemies. Such inhumanity contravenes God's law and must be punished. Israel probably rejoiced at the fall of this enemy!

Ammon greedy for more territory, fought to enlarge their borders and not just in self-defence. They resorted to great cruelty to gain their ends, injuring pregnant women and blinding their captives. They too were guilty and due for judgment.

Philistia and Phoenicia (or Tyre), were judged guilty of slave trading. Philistia raided other nations purely to get human prisoners and took whole nations captive as slaves. Phoenicia and Edom were involved in this bartering for human lives and were to be judged accordingly. For this Israel would be glad!

Edom, springing from Esau whose 'anger raged continually' after the loss of his birth-right, was judged for having no pity or compassion. They contravened all the laws of love and forgiveness. Read Isaiah 63 to see that God offered no mercy to Edom.

Moab. From Judges 3:12; 1 Samuel 14:47; 2 Samuel 8:2 we see there was great enmity between Moab and Israel. Was it in defiance of Israel's God that Moab burned the bones of kings? To deny there was any existence after death? To desecrate what was reverenced by another nation?

Judah. From the map you will see Amos had dealt with all the nations on the east, north and south of Israel. In coming to Judah he now completely circumscribed Israel. Judah's sin was that in turning from the true God, she now worshipped the idols of Canaan. Judah refused to keep God's law and spurned His help, forgetting that He had delivered them from Egypt.

Israel. Did Israel smugly think she would escape Amos' message? Her sin was very great. All the more so because, as God's covenant people, she should have known better. She could have been a godly witness to the nations around. The Israelites stood condemned. They sold human beings; their law courts were corrupt; greed, heartlessness and disrespect for other people were rife. They worshipped in heathen temples, indulged in prostitution and broke the law of God over and over again. Had they forgotten Egypt and God's great faithfulness to them? Now they silenced the prophets and desecrated the Nazarites and did not want to be reminded of God's holy standards.

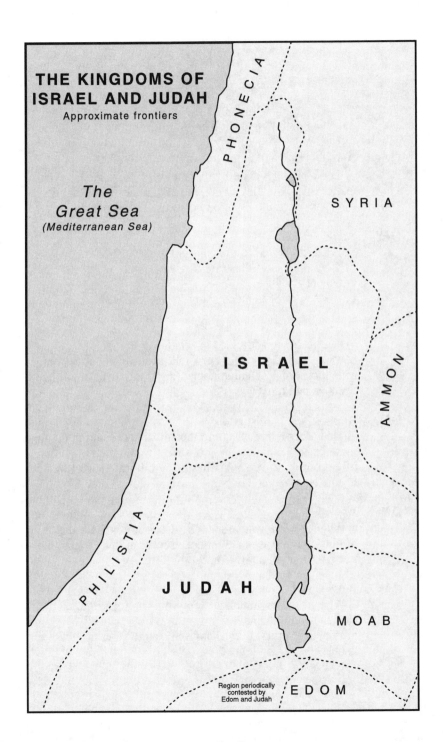

THE KINGDOMS OF
ISRAEL AND JUDAH
Approximate frontiers

PHONECIA

The
Great Sea
(Mediterranean Sea)

SYRIA

ISRAEL

AMMON

PHILISTIA

JUDAH

MOAB

Region periodically
contested by
Edom and Judah

EDOM

STUDY 3
PRIVILEGE AND ITS PERILS

QUESTIONS

DAY 1 *Amos 1:3, 6, 7, 11, 13.*
a) Look back at some of the sins of these nations. What modern-day atrocities have some nations been guilty of today?
b) What sins can our nation be accused of (Amos 2:4)?

DAY 2 *Amos 2:9-16.*
a) What has added to the guilt of Israel (vv. 9-12)?
b) How does God illustrate the inevitability of the coming judgment (vv. 14-16)?
c) What are we reminded about in Hebrews 2:3?

DAY 3 *Amos 3:1-2.*
a) Who is being addressed in verse 1?
b) What had the people been told about their relationship with the Lord in Deuteronomy 7:6-11? And what had they been warned to do?

DAY 4 *Amos 3:2-6.*
a) How does Amos illustrate the law of cause and effect in these verses?
b) According to verse 6, what is the biblical view of world history?

DAY 5 *Amos 3:7-8.*
a) Why was Amos able to speak out God's words to the nation?
b) In what way was his experience similar to that of Jeremiah (Jer. 20:9), and Paul (1 Cor. 9:16)?

DAY 6 *Amos 3:9-11.*
a) Where did Israel think her loot would be secure? What did God say about this?
b) Why in Matthew 6:19-21 are we urged to store up treasure in heaven?

QUESTIONS (contd.)

DAY 7 *Amos 3:12-15.*
a) What reason is again given for the coming punishment?
b) What elements in this prophecy would give rise to both despair and hope among the people?

MEMORY VERSE: Amos 3:2

NOTES

To help us understand Israel's situation we start with Abraham stepping out on God's promises (Gen. 12:1-2). His family grows and Jacob, later called 'Israel', becomes leader. Israel and his family go to Egypt where Joseph, the young brother whom they thought they had killed (Gen. 37), was Prime Minister. He provided for them in a time of famine and they became a large and prosperous people.

Pharaoh is afraid of their increasing strength and seeks to suppress them (Exod. 1:8-12). Moses is directed by God to lead Israel out of Egypt and away from Pharaoh's tyranny (Exod. 3:10) about 1,290 years before Christ's birth. Joshua leads the people into the Promised Land of Canaan, where they are ruled by prophets and judges until Samuel's time. The nation then asks Samuel to give them a king like the nations round about (1 Sam. 8:5).

King Saul, David and Solomon all reign in succession until 925 BC when the Kingdom divides into Judah (capital – Jerusalem) and Israel (capital – Samaria). Soon after this, Amos comes on the scene (about 721 BC). He lived in the southern Kingdom of Judah between Jerusalem and Bethlehem. It was from here that he started to speak God's Word to the nations.

In chapter 3 of Amos, Israel is being reminded that God had set His favour on them, delivering and protecting them. All down the years God had stressed that Israel was to be a holy, separate people (Deut. 14:2), warning them not to fraternise with the idolatrous people around them (Deut. 13:12-18). But Israel now ignored her privilege, took God's blessings for granted and for their personal gain, and neglected their responsibility to be true to God and a holy witness to other nations (see chapter 9:10).

Amos now pointed out how wrong they were. No doubt they questioned his message and ridiculed a mere shepherd, doubting if he could be the mouthpiece of God. But Amos (3:3) stresses he is one with God in His purposes and that God, as surely as a lion descends on its prey (v. 4), and the unwary bird is snared (v. 5), and that the sound of the trumpet brings disaster (v. 6), is warning faithless Israel of judgment to come.

God's voice has come through many humble servants down through the generations and still today, despite all our privileges, He warns us that we are answerable to a God of love and holiness, for the way we live. John 15:16 says, 'You did not choose me, but I chose you ...'

Someone has said: 'Watch television with the sound turned off. You'll soon see that action without comment easily becomes meaningless and open to any kind of interpretation.' This is why God has provided His Word through His prophets, disciples and apostles, to explain His actions and direct us in our Christian walk.

Just as Amos was compelled to give the Israelites the Word of God, so the Apostles (see Acts 4:20), when they were told to stop preaching about Jesus said, 'we cannot help speaking about what we have seen and heard.' There was that inner compulsion to speak out the truth.

STUDY 4
PRETENCE DOESN'T PAY

QUESTIONS

DAY 1 *Amos 4:1-3.*
a) Why might Amos have called these women 'cows'?
b) What sins were they guilty of?
c) 'A chain is only as strong as its weakest link.' Discuss the key role that can be played by women in today's society.

DAY 2 *Amos 4:4-5; 1 Kings 12:26-33.*
How had Jeroboam (not the Jeroboam who was living in Amos' day) given a boost to false worship at Bethel?

DAY 3 *Amos 4:4-5.*
a) Why might the people have thought God would have been pleased with them?
b) What attitude of the people indicates that there was something wrong with their religion? (Jesus rebuked a similar attitude in Matthew 6:1,5.)

DAY 4 *Amos 4:6-11.*
a) What is God complaining about here?
b) How does God act towards His children today (Heb. 12:5-6)?

DAY 5 *Amos 4:12.*
a) What were the people called upon to do?
b) Why were they called upon to do this?

DAY 6 *Amos 4:12.*
a) What encounter are we warned to prepare for in Acts 17:31?
b) How can we prepare for this (John 5:24)? Why should we be ready now?

DAY 7 *Amos 4:13.*
a) Why were the people reminded of this description of God?
b) Take time to meditate on what God says about Himself.

MEMORY VERSE: Amos 4:13

Amos here opens a real barrage in Israel and exposes the nation's sin and shame unmercifully. He attacks the self-indulgent rich women, calling them fat cows (such were the cattle fed on the rich pasture lands of Bashan) who lived just for themselves. They influenced their husbands to be ruthless in business. It was just too bad for the 'under-dog' – they must have money for their comfort and pleasure. They used people because of their love of things. God wants us to love people and use things to help them. Amos points out that all must be judged and face death no matter how high (or humble) their station in life.

He exposes their hypocrisy in religion. They appeared to be giving God His due but Amos saw through the sham, as God did, and Malachi (Mal. 1:7-8). What a shock when God opens the eyes of people to their rotten self-centredness! But if God speaks and we respond this can lead to blessing and deliverance. These people were so steeped in religion and acting as if they were God-centred that they were even fooling themselves. When we give in to Satan and self, God is not, nor can He be, first. We really make gods of ourselves just as Satan tempted Adam and Eve to do in Genesis 3:5. The Geared for Growth study on Freedom looks at this in much more detail (see Romans 6). Do we need to stock-take and pray that the Holy Spirit will reveal to us whether God or some other worthless, selfish thing is at the centre of our lives?

God had been so good to Israel all these years. If only they had sung:

Count your blessings, count them one by one,
Count your blessings, see what God has done.
Count your blessings, name them one by one,
And it will surprise you what the Lord has done.

But God's judgment was coming. Amos knew the people weren't ready to meet God (vv. 5, 18). They had lost the awareness of God's matchless holiness and had forgotten that He wanted them to be a holy people. They had indulged in selfish and sinful ways for so long and yet blatantly enjoyed His blessings that they probably thought that God, like a kindly old grandad, would wink at their sins and welcome them into Heaven anyway. So Amos impresses on them again the greatness and holiness of the great 'I am' of Israel.

How patient and long-suffering God is. Because of His love He won't leave us alone. He sees how easily we can be lulled into indifference by the devil's lies, so stirs us by testings and trials and sometimes hardships to make us realise our peril. He shook the Israelites through the prophets because He loved them. And this great patient God still speaks to us today, convicting us of sin, calling us through His Word and by His Spirit to repent, sometimes sending trials and difficulties into our lives when we stubbornly refuse to yield to His love.

Today Thy mercy calls me, to wash away my sin,
However great my trespass, whate'er I might have been.
However long from mercy I may have turned away,
Thy blood, O Christ, can cleanse me and make me pure today.

STUDY 5
AN INVITATION TO LIVE

QUESTIONS

DAY 1 *Amos 5:1-3.*
a) Why are these verses described as a 'lament' or 'dirge'?
b) Why would there be no one to lift Israel up?

DAY 2 *Amos 5:4-6.*
a) What did the people have to choose between?
b) Who could the people blame if they went into exile?

DAY 3 *Amos 5:7-13.*
a) Who were suffering at the hands of the people?
b) What was God's general verdict on the people in verse 12a?

DAY 4 *Amos 5:14-15.*
a) In what way had the people been deluding themselves?
b) What kind of life does Jesus offer us in John 10:10, 27-28?

DAY 5 *Amos 5:16-17.*
a) What similarities exist between these verses and Exodus 12:12, 29-30?
b) What kind of sorrow is depicted in Matthew 13:40-43, 47-49?

DAY 6 *Amos 5:18-20.*
a) Under what delusion were some people living?
b) How do these verses illustrate the truth of Hebrews 2:3a?

DAY 7 *Amos 5:21-27.*
a) What was God's verdict on their religious rituals?
b) What should they have learned from 1 Samuel 15:22-23?
c) Why is it important to distrust our own opinions on salvation (Prov. 16:25)?

MEMORY VERSE: Amos 5:4

NOTES

Amos, walking closely with God, knew that God had to deal with Israel's sin. Because he saw how Israel was living in defiance of God's laws and making a sham of true worship, he felt that already her fate was sealed and God's judgment was upon them. So he speaks as if the blow had already fallen.

He underlines clearly that despite their fraternising with the other nations (in slave trade, etc.) these nations wouldn't stand by Israel when the chips were down. She was debilitated by her own luxurious living too and when an attack came she would have little resources with which to counteract it. How true are the words from 'Onward Christian Soldiers' – 'The arm of flesh will fail you; you dare not trust your own.'

Amos points out too the futility of a false religion. It was no use going to the 'altars of God' and putting on an outward show when their hearts were steeped in sin. David said in Psalm 24:3-6 that we can only approach God if we have clean hands and a pure heart. I Corinthians 11:29 warns us, especially in the light of the meaning of the communion service, of the danger of worshipping with unconfessed and uncleansed sin in our hearts. The evidence of a heart right with God is a life and conduct that shows this. If we worship the Lord 'in spirit and in truth' our lives will show the fruit of the Spirit (Gal. 5:22-25). The lives of the Israelites were corrupt, so what point was there in going through the show of worship?

God's great heart of love is glimpsed through Amos' reiteration of 'Seek the LORD and live.' How often God had dealt in patience with Israel. How often He had raised up righteous men to lead them and teach them His law. How constantly He yearned over them, likening Himself to the protective mother hen who gathers her helpless chicks under her covering wings (Matt. 23:37). If only the Israelites would have prayed sincerely:

Oh spread Thy covering wings around till all our wanderings cease,
And at our Father's loved abode, our souls arrive in peace.

There is a day of reckoning coming. Amos warns Israel that she had to meet her God. His chosen people should have been looking to that day with expectancy and gladness. No doubt they even felt complacent, not realising that their sin could only bring condemnation and death when Christ appeared. We are so strongly urged to be cleansed from sin and know peace with God so that we can look with glad expectancy for His coming again.

This whole chapter speaks of self-satisfaction and hypocrisy. The great Father-God is powerless to bless while they persist in sin. He is the God of Hosts, splendid in His holiness, so the consequences of Israel's sin and folly must come upon them.

How thankful we should be that God's mercy and grace are available to us today. How diligent we should be in bringing others to know Him. Every soul is God's by right of Creation and Redemption, but so many are still held captive by Satan and sin. May we be burdened to pray for others.

Oh come, Oh come Immanuel and rescue captive Israel ...
Oh come, Thou rod of Jesse, free Thine own from Satan's tyranny.
From depths of hell, Thy people save and give them victory o'er the grave
Oh come, Thou King of David come, and open wide Thy heavenly home.
Make safe the way that leads on high and close the paths to misery...
Rejoice, Rejoice, Immanuel shall come, to Thee, oh Israel.

STUDY 6
DANGER – MEN ASLEEP!

QUESTIONS

DAY 1 *Amos 6:1, 4-6, 13.*
a) What must have lulled these national leaders into a false sense of security?
b) Had their own strength got them to Canaan? How should they have been boasting (Jer. 9:23-24)?

DAY 2 *Amos 6:4-6; James 2:14-19.*
a) How were these leaders spending their money?
b) What should they have been concerned about?
c) What does the 'James' reference say about true faith?

DAY 3 *Amos 6:4-6.*
a) What aspects of David's life had the people forgotten to emulate (Ps. 63)?
b) Can music be a help or a distraction in our worship of God?

DAY 4 *Amos 6:7-11.*
a) What result will Israel's indifference and folly bring?
b) Why would these things definitely happen (v. 8)?

DAY 5 *Amos 6:12.*
The warped sense of justice of the nation is compared to poison. What forms of poison do you see infecting our nation today?

DAY 6 *Amos 6:14.*
a) How does this verse contrast with 2 Kings 14:23-26?
b) Which way is the most profitable in the long term: God's way or ours (Prov. 16:25)?

DAY 7 *Genesis 12:1-3; James 1:17.*
a) What was God's promise to Abraham and his descendants?
b) Is God changeable? Could He have been blamed for failing Israel?
c) Can we trust Him completely (Jude 1:24)?

MEMORY VERSE: Amos 6:8

God's blessings to Israel were fast becoming a curse because they were being used selfishly. The nation now took for granted that, since they were chosen of God, then automatically only good would come to them. God's promises are always conditional. His holy standard must be kept. And here Israel fails miserably.

Men who, under God, should have been vital leaders and champions of God's cause, influenced the nation to self-indulgence and pride. At peace with her neighbours and financially secure, she should have been improving the lot of the lower classes. Instead the poor were exploited and the rich got richer, indulging themselves in extravagant living. They became self-sufficient and hard of heart, boasting of their national and military powers as if God had not been their guide and deliverer.

What a warning to His children to remember the goodness of God, to walk humbly and to fulfil faithfully the responsibilities entrusted to us. There is also a warning red light flashing here telling us to walk, not with our eyes on men, however godly, but looking or fixing 'our eyes on Jesus' as Hebrews 12:2 puts it.

While Israel played the fool and relaxed (feeling 'secure' as v. 1 says), virtually fulfilling Jeremiah 8:11, '"Peace, peace," they say, when there is no peace,' God was saying through Amos, 'I despise the pride of Jacob and false glory of Israel, and hate their beautiful homes. I will turn over this city and everything in it to her enemies' (Amos 6:8, LB).

Verses 7-10 indicate that Israel's oppressions would force her into exile and the first to go would be those who had led her in her folly. All that they had acquired would be destroyed or go to their conquerors. The few who survived the war would die from a plague. Whole families would be wiped out and there would be so many dead they would have to be burned rather than buried. Survivors would be afraid to mention God's name in case further judgment fell. Oh, the tragedy of wasted opportunity! How tragic that a people whom God purposed to be a blessing to the nations should, like Esau, despise their birth-right, throwing the companionship of God aside for a few baubles which would soon be destroyed anyway.

Israel *knew* better, but she refused to *do* better.

What a tremendous challenge this is to us to earnestly covet all that God has for us and not to seek satisfaction in trivialities. Someone has aptly said, 'If you are called to be a servant of God, don't stoop to be a king.'

Oh Master, when Thou callest no voice may say Thee nay,
For blest are they that follow where Thou dost lead the way.
In freshest prime of morning or fullest glow of noon,
The note of heavenly warning can never come too soon.

STUDY 7
PLEADING WITH GOD

QUESTIONS

DAY 1 *Amos 7:1-3.*
a) Why did Amos become very upset?
b) Why did God not carry out His threat?

DAY 2 *Amos 7:3-6.*
a) What does Amos now see?
b) How did he react to this vision?

DAY 3 *Amos 7:1-6.*
a) What important ingredients of prayer does Amos demonstrate?
b) What is Jesus said to do for believers in Hebrews 7:25; I John 2:1?
c) What did Paul urge as important in I Timothy 2:1-3,8?

DAY 4 *Amos 7:7-9; Isaiah 28:17.*
a) What does God's use of the plumb-line suggest about His justice?
b) Against what false standards could we be comparing ourselves?

DAY 5 *Amos 7:10-13.*
a) What apparent misconceptions did Amaziah have about Amos? (Were they excuses to avoid his message?)
b) What excuses ('red herrings') do we sometimes use to avoid facing up to truth?

DAY 6 *Amos 7:14-16;*
a) Why did Amos refuse to stop preaching? What message did he have for Amaziah?
b) Amos may have been tempted to doubt but remembered God's word to him. What doubts can the following verses help us defeat: John 6:37; Galatians 1:11; Hebrews 11:6? Take time to share other verses that have helped you.

DAY 7 *Amos 7:17.*
What particular prophecy did Amos have for Amaziah?

MEMORY VERSE: Amos 7:2, 4

Proverbs 29:18 says, 'Where there is no vision, the people perish' (AV). Amos' heart beat at one with God's. Thus God was able to communicate His message to the Israelites through Amos. In a series of visions, God's judgments on Israel are further clarified to Amos. First he sees the locust plague which would be of such intensity that national survival would be out of the question, followed by one of fire or drought which would destroy the land itself. He pleads that God won't allow this to happen and God hears his prayer. Can we pause and ask ourselves here what our vision is? How closely do we live to God? What is the burden of our prayer?

Then God appears in the role of a Master Builder to inspect the work of His workmen. He has made provision (guidance of His law) for the work (spiritual growth of the nation) and had come to assess what had been done. The New Testament reveals to us that the law was done away with in Christ and full provision is made for us today in the finished work of Christ on Calvary. By His grace we can be righteous and doing works of righteousness, so that we don't all fall short of God's measure. Read further on this in Romans 3:19-26; 7:7-13; 8:1-4; Galatians 3:21-29. It would be terrible if God had to meet us with the assessment which he delivered to King Belshazzar in Daniel 5:27: 'You have been weighed on the scales and found wanting'.

We see in these verses too the mighty power of the Word of God. It came in such conviction ('Sharper than any double-edged sword' – Heb. 4:12) that the priest of Bethel and Jeroboam, in an attempt to stifle it, decided to try and get rid of the one who spoke it. But we see that Amos' confidence in God's word enabled him to prophesy with boldness. In Luke 4 we see that Christ used God's Word to refute the devil. We, too, have full provision made through God's Word to be 'more than conquerors' both in our personal walk and in battling for souls (Eph. 6:17). It is interesting to note, too, that men, especially men under conviction, are quick to belittle the messenger who delivers that word, just as they despised Christ, the Word made flesh, who appeared for their salvation (John 1:14; Isa. 53:3).

Amos was unperturbed by their accusations. Convinced that God had called him for the task (Amos 7:15) he got on with it faithfully. If we look at the life of Paul, we see that he preached with a similar authority, fearing no-one (1 Cor. 15:10; Gal. 1:15-16; Eph. 3:7, 9; 1 Tim. 1:12-16). Amos did not sit and mope because he was a simple shepherd and therefore not equipped for the task; no more did Paul boast in all his background and education as his credentials for preaching. Both knew that their ministry was by the grace of God.

Another aspect of Amos' ministry which comes through here is the ministry of prayer.

He was stirred by the words of Amaziah in chapter 7:10,14. But he was righteously stirred. Amaziah, in opposing Amos, was really opposing God. It is an issue of God's word against a man's word. But Amos stood his ground for he knew God must act in justice and judgment. However, Amos doesn't just preach destruction. He prays for Israel's deliverance. In chapter 7:3-6 it says that God 'relented'. But God is unchangeable; how could He relent? Amos was the repentant one, standing in Israel's place, or where Israel would have stood if she had repented. His prayer for Israel meant that another side of God's character was shown. No, God hadn't changed. But Israel, in Amos, had. Here we touch on the mystery of prayer. As Amos prayed on Israel's behalf, God withheld judgment.

But don't forget, at a much deeper level, God had prepared an Amos who would pray.

The picture brings sharply into focus God's wonderful provision for our redemption. Before we ever lived He had prepared the Lamb of God to be our 'stand in' before God (Rev. 13:8). Scripture says, 'God was reconciling the world to himself in Christ' (2 Cor. 5:19). Moses was willing to forego the eternal presence of God if only his people could be saved (Exod. 32:30). Jesus very definitely took our place on Calvary, bearing the wrath and rejection of God, that we might go free. In the strength of this intercession (life outpoured) He now lives to continually intercede for us (Heb. 7:25). Likewise we as His children are called to 'pray without ceasing' and to give ourselves in self-sacrificial living and devotion to God (Rom. 12:1-2).

STUDY 8

WE REAP WHAT WE SOW

QUESTIONS

DAY 1 *Amos 8:1-3.*
a) What was Amos to learn from this vision?
b) Why do you think there were many bodies in the temple?
c) What do these verses say about God's patience: Romans 2:4; 1 Peter 3:20; 2 Peter 3:15?

DAY 2 *Amos 8:4-6.*
a) How were these merchants being dishonest?
b) How were they also being hypocritical?

DAY 3 *Amos 8:7-8.*
a) What are we reminded about God?
b) To what is the upheavel caused by the coming judgment compared?

DAY 4 *Amos 8:9-10.*
a) How is the deep sorrow the people would endure depicted?
b) What kind of grieving is mentioned in 1 Thessalonians 4:13?

DAY 5 *Amos 8:11-12.*
a) What tragic kind of famine is now predicted?
b) Why is God's Word more important than even our daily food (Ps. 119:9, 103, 105, 130; Matt. 4:4; 1 Pet. 1:22)? Do you think we would appreciate it more if we were denied access to it?

DAY 6 *Amos 8:13-14.*
a) Who would suffer from thirst?
b) Why would the people not have a right to blame God for all that would happen?

DAY 7 *Luke 16:19-31.*
What comparisons can you find between this rich man and the nation of Israel in Amos 8?

MEMORY VERSE: Amos 8:11

NOTES

I remember singing as a child – 'Sow flowers and flowers will blossom around you wherever you go. Sow weeds and of weeds reap the harvest; you reap whatsoever you sow.'

This chapter is a picture of Israel reaping what she had sown in disobedience and defiance of God. In Jeremiah 8:20 we read, 'The harvest is past, the summer has ended, and we are not saved'. It was this verse that brought me to a realisation of my personal need and ultimately to put my faith in Christ the Redeemer. Israel has come to a crossroads in her experience. She has deliberately closed her heart and mind to the pleadings of a loving and patient, but Holy, God. Now He must act, to preserve His Holy Name, and ultimately to save Israel from final destruction.

He shows Amos in a vision a 'basket of ripe fruit'. Whether this indicates the end of summer and the beginning of the autumn season when there is no further growth, or fruit that is over-ripe, the resulting picture is the same. Apparently Amos used a play on words here, as the word KAITZ (summer fruit) and KETZ (the end) are almost the same. God was indicating that spiritual decay in the nation must have an end.

We glimpse something of the rottenness of sin in the lives of these people and understand a little of just why God must deal with them as He does. God's judgment is pronounced on them because of their blatant disregard for His law. This manifests itself, as we have seen before, in innate selfishness and greed. In the verses in question we see that in trading they defrauded others in order to feather their own nests. They made the measuring pan smaller, thus selling the people short. The panier, in which goods were weighed, was fitted with a false base, again to give short measure for the money paid. A shekel was used to weigh so much cash and by increasing its weight they defrauded their clients, who obviously had to add more to balance the scales. These measures resulted in the poor being really hard-pressed and forced less fortunate businessmen into bankruptcy. Their greed even affected their attitude to the 'Lord's Day' as they just couldn't wait for the Sabbath to pass till they could begin their evil practices. They had come a long way from the command to remember to keep the Sabbath Day holy.

So Israel was to be judged because she was trampling ruthlessly on the law of God which set out such standards as 'put God first', 'love your neighbour', 'do not steal', and was living entirely to gratify herself and not to glorify God.

There was to come upon them a period when they would have nothing but silence from God. Can you imagine how terrible society would be with no Bibles, no churches, no minister, no fellowship, no Christian standards, no restraints on wickedness? Can you imagine a generation brought up without the influence of the Word of God on their lives?

What a desolate picture! Maybe we would dare to say, 'How could God allow such a thing?' But so often God has to speak very loudly through seemingly adverse situations to bring us to our senses. As these studies are being prepared I think of the famine and sickness in Africa. Terrible? Yes, but at least the world's attention is now focusing on the area of need – Christians are on the alert seeking to pour in supplies. Is this God's way to open the door wide for the gospel and ultimate salvation for these people?

The temples, where God should have been worshipped and His praises sung, had become centres of idolatry. Because they had profaned His house, their songs were now to be turned to wails of distress. Instead of the joy of 'Harvest Thanksgiving', there was to be mourning and sorrow. God foretells they would bury their dead in silence. Sulking or submitting? How do you react to God's rebukes? Surely they were beginning to see that selfishness and sin don't bring a pleasant reward. We are warned that the wages of sin is death.

Yet God, while acting in judgment, longed for a change of heart from His people. He did purpose to save them. He did purpose to bless His people and make them a blessing. Malachi 4:2 says, 'But for you who revere my name, the sun of righteousness will rise with healing in its wings'. Isaiah 61 tells of the promised Messiah, the One who would come to wipe away their tears and turn their mourning into joy. In 2 Peter 3:9 we read that God is unwilling that any of us should perish.

Israel's lot should caution us to make sure our hearts are right with God. Our desire should be to live, not for personal gain, but for the furtherance of God's Kingdom. Matthew 6:33 tells us to seek this first and all the other needs of life will fall into place. If the women in Amos' days had not been influencing their men to tax the poor to satisfy their greed, perhaps this state of affairs would never have existed. Are we lovers of the Lord Jesus, satisfied with Him and laying up treasure in Heaven (Matt. 6:19-20)?

Lay up treasure in Heaven; life will pass away,
Lay up treasure in abundant measure for the great accounting day,
Lay up treasure in Heaven – though men count thee poor,
Thou shalt live with the Sons of God – forever more.

STUDY 9
A BLACK PICTURE

QUESTIONS

DAY 1 *Amos 9:1.*
a) Why was an altar essential to the worship of God (Lev. 9:7)?
b) What did God tell Amos was going to happen? When might this have been at least partially fulfilled (Amos 1:1)?

DAY 2 *Amos 9:2-4; Psalm 139:7-10.*
a) How are the efforts of the people to escape God's judgment portrayed?
b) Why would these efforts be futile?

DAY 3 *Amos 9:2-4; Revelation 6:15-17.*
a) What similarities exist between the 'Amos' and 'Revelation' references?
b) Genesis 3:8-13. After sinning, what did Adam and Eve try and fail to do?

DAY 4 *Amos 9:5-6.*
a) What simple act of God affects all the earth (v. 5; Ps. 104:32)?
b) How should we respond to God's revelation of Himself (Jer. 5:24)?

DAY 5 *Amos 9:7.*
a) How does God rebuke their national pride?
b) What false hope must they have been living under?

DAY 6 *Amos 9:8.*
a) How is the nation again described?
b) Contrast this verse with Psalm 33:18-19. What happens to each group God observes?

DAY 7 *Amos 9:8-10.*
a) To what is God's judgment compared?
b) What hope for the future is introduced?
c) Who would not escape?

MEMORY VERSE: Amos 9:8b.

Did Amos' vision of God in the temple raise his hopes that God would again relent and bless? God's words soon convinced Amos otherwise. He had come to destroy. The chief sanctuary of Bethel had already been made a centre of idol worship. God now commanded it to be stricken till it collapsed upon those within. Historians say this was probably brought about by an earthquake.

If any escaped destruction when the temple fell and sought refuge in Sheol (the place of the dead), or in mountain caves ('climb up to the heavens', v. 2), or at the bottom of the sea (v. 3), God would lay hold of them. Deportation to a foreign country wouldn't put them beyond the reach of God, for they and their captors would be slain.

There would be no escape now that Israel, in defiance of God's holy law, had fallen into the hands of the living God (Heb. 10:31). God had set His eye on them for evil, and not for good (v. 4).

We see in verse 6 that God is in control of the universe and every living creature. Israel claimed superiority to other nations because of God's favour on them as His chosen people. They wrongly assumed that nothing adverse could happen to them because God was God and could not fail. God points out through Amos (vv. 7-8) that He directs the life of every nation and that Israel, despite His favour, must suffer the consequence of her sin. This chapter clearly reveals the omnipotence (all-powerful) and omnipresence (ever present) of a Sovereign God (a God in full control). Israel, of necessity, must be judged the more drastically for her sin, because she had been taught God's law, but this privilege also carried the greater responsibility of obeying God and manifesting Him in righteousness to other nations (see Study 3).

Throughout this book we see that God assesses His children on the level of their works. Refer again to I Corinthians 3:13 and 2 Corinthians 5:10-11. These, and many more scriptures, point out the futility of saying one thing and doing another. Someone has aptly put it: 'Your life speaks so loudly, I cannot hear what you say'. Matthew 7:16 says that men are known by what their lives produce.

The Israelites professed to be God's people but their lives produced 'the works of the flesh' (Gal. 5:19-21, AV) and not the 'fruit of the Spirit' (Gal. 5:22-26). Revelation 3:15 puts God's searchlight right on the Church of Christ. Does this scripture search your heart? We are reminded that we are, as His children, temples of the living God (I Cor. 3:16). Surely the place where God dwells must be worthy of Him? No works of righteousness that we can do will make us fit for God (Titus 3:5). We stand only through faith in Christ's atoning work. Only out of such a 'faith relationship' (outlined in John 15 as the 'abiding life') can the 'fruit of the Spirit' result. Israel did not 'dwell closely' to God. She greedily went after what she wanted and reaped the reward. May this study encourage us to make sure our foundations are right, that we 'keep living in Christ' and our lives keep producing the good things (love, joy, peace, gentleness, etc.) which manifest Christ's life within us.

We are building day by day, as the moments pass away,
A temple which the world cannot see,
Every vict'ry won by grace will be sure to find a place
In that building for eternity.

STUDY 10
A PROMISING FUTURE

QUESTIONS

DAY 1 *Amos 9:11-15.*
What words are used to indicate that God's judgment of the nation would be severe?

DAY 2 *Amos 5:11, 16, 27; 9:11-15.*
a) What effects of the nation's sin and judgment did God promise specifically to undo?
b) What effects of sin will not be found in heaven according to Revelation 21:4?

DAY 3 *Amos 9:11-15.*
a) What evidence is there from current events to suggest that this prophecy is being fulfilled for Israel today?
b) What words suggest that this prophecy may have more than a literal fulfilment?

DAY 4 *Amos 9:12; Isaiah 9:6-7; 11:10; 60:2-3.*
a) Who are affected by any restoration of Israel?
b) Who is the Person who reigns in Isaiah 9:6-7?

DAY 5 *Acts 15:1-22.*
a) Why was this Council being held at Jerusalem?
b) Which verse is a quotation from Amos?
b) What link did James (v. 13) see between Amos' prophecy and the conversion of the Gentiles?

DAY 6 *Amos 9:11.*
a) How might these verses encourage us if we feel our lives have been damaged by sin?
b) What is God's promise to us in 1 John 1:9?

DAY 7 *Amos 1:1-2.*
a) Whose words are referred to in this verse? Glance through Amos again. Who really has spoken in this book?
b) Why can we trust these 'words of Amos' (2 Pet. 1:20-21)?

MEMORY VERSE: Amos 9:14-15

NOTES

Israel had certainly 'acted like a fool' as Saul also acknowledged that he had (I Sam. 26:21). All who stand and act in their own wisdom and in independence of God are included under this category (Rom. 1:22). Yet God says He will not utterly destroy. He will judge, but He will restore. His divine plan is to save. This is why the Messiah is promised to Israel and a Redeemer to mankind. From the remnant saved at this time of God's judgment would come this 'seed of David' (Luke 1:31-33).

Amos sees, beyond God's drastic dealings, a day of hope dawning for Israel. Verses 11-12 show that Israel will again rise and overcome her enemies in the power of God (v. 12, 'the LORD who will do these things').

All the devastation of this day will be made good. Above all, the tabernacle would be rebuilt, indicating God once again in the midst of an obedient people. With priorities right, the resultant picture of harmony between them and God would be a witness to the nations (Isa. 2:2-5).

The picture becomes increasingly rosy as these verses unfold. The produce of the land will be so prolific that all the crop won't be gathered before it is time to sow again. God's provision would be so abundant that it would seem the rivers flowed with wine! No sign of poverty or need here. God's promised provision (and here we think not just about material things, but all our spiritual needs) for His children is good measure, pressed down and running over (Luke 6:38). 'And my God will meet all your needs according to his glorious riches in Christ Jesus' (Phil. 4:19).

The picture in verse 14 is one of restoration and blessing. Read the story of the prodigal son in Luke 15:11-32. Here we get a clear revelation of the love and mercy of God: His patience in waiting till we come to our senses, repent and confess our waywardness and sin and return to His loving care.

God's glorious sovereign hand is in control. The interplay of His purposes (divine sovereignty) coming to bear on human hearts is clearly seen in the simple 'I will ... they will'. Surely there is an echo here from 2 Corinthians 5:14, 'For Christ's love compels us ...'. Written into these few pages in the history of Israel are profound truths which are strongly re-echoed through the New Testament and fully applicable in our day and generation.

The fact of sin must be dealt with. God's judgment must come, not for revenge, but to preserve His holy standards. Since all have sinned and are guilty and due for judgment, He has provided the way of repentance and faith through Christ's atoning work (Rom. 8:2) and deals in mercy and love with the heart that turns to Him. The blessings of His salvation are ours to enjoy now and throughout eternity. How is His 'restoration work' in your life progressing?

God is working His purposes out
As year succeeds to year:
God is working His purposes out
And the time is drawing near
Nearer, nearer draws the time
The time that shall surely be,
When the earth shall be filled with the Glory of God,
As the waters cover the sea.

ANSWER GUIDE

The following pages contain an Answer Guide. It is recommended that answers to the questions be attempted before turning to this guide. It is only a guide and the answers given should not be treated as exhaustive.

GUIDE TO INTRODUCTORY STUDY

Read this Introductory Study together. Look up and discuss the references before proceeding to Study I.

Remember Amos is a book in which God warns and exposes sin and disobedience in His people, and paints a solemn picture of how He must deal with sin since He is a Holy God. It is God's Word. But beyond the black clouds is the rainbow of God's promise – always there for those who will hear, heed and obey His voice, for He always plans in love for His people (Zeph. 3:17, original translation).

GUIDE TO STUDY 1

DAY 1 a) He was a shepherd from the Southern Kingdom of Judah as Tekoa is just south of Bethlehem.
b) He probably saw for himself the moral and religious state of Israel; God also revealed to him His threats against Israel: He had heard God roar in judgment.

DAY 2 a) God had allowed him to expand the boundaries of Israel; he enjoyed a long reign; the nation's suffering had come to an end.
b) A negative influence as he himself still followed evil practices (2 Kings. 14:24).

DAY 3 a) He took care of sycamore (fig) trees.
b) He might have sold his wool and fruit there.

DAY 4 a) God deliberately called him.
b) No.

DAY 5 a) Yes – but it was not a religion that was pleasing to God.
b) Very sinful. It was dominated by injustice, oppression, incestuous relationships and self-gratification at the expense of others.

DAY 6 Rebellious, idolatrous and sinful.

DAY 7 Israel would suffer judgment and exile but would later be restored to her own land.

GUIDE TO STUDY 2

DAY 1 a) We always take delight in seeing our enemies being denounced.
b) Because of her excessive cruelty to others. The 'Kings' references list some of her crimes.
c) Through the king of Assyria later attacking Syria.

DAY 2 a) Because of ethnic cleansing in deporting whole communities to a country renowned for its cruelty.
b) That between Hiram king of Tyre and king Solomon.

DAY 3 a) Determined and revengeful unforgiveness.
b) God is a God of forgiveness.
c) Only 'righteous' anger can be justified. Prolonged periods of anger are to be avoided.

DAY 4 a) Her greed to gain fresh territory.
b) The danger of covetousness as it leads to self-destruction and great sorrow.

DAY 5 a) The burning of a king's bones.
That nothing we do is hidden from God's gaze.
b) Her arrogance, pride and defiance of God.

DAY 6 a) Judah had despised God's law, broken His commandments and been led astray by false gods.
b) Carefully listen to it and obey its teachings.

DAY 7 a) They are now being rebuked by God.
b) Injustice, prostitution, greed and heartlessness.

AMOS • ANSWER GUIDE

GUIDE TO STUDY 3

DAY 1
a) Massacres in Cambodia, Rwanda, Bosnia, etc.
b) Personal.

DAY 2
a) Her disregard of God's past favours to her and her deliberate refusal to listen to any warnings (through the prophets).
b) Those people most likely to succeed or escape in battle will not be able to.
c) There is no escape for neglecting salvation.

DAY 3
a) Both the nations of Israel and Judah.
b) That in His love and mercy God had specially chosen them as His own.
To follow carefully all the laws God had given them.

DAY 4
a) The walking together, the roaring of the lion, the trap springing, the people trembling are all due to previous events occurring.
b) God is behind every event in world history.

DAY 5
a) God had revealed it to him.
b) Like Jeremiah and Paul he was unable to be silent and felt compelled to speak out.

DAY 6
a) In her fortresses.
God said they would be plundered.
b) Our only abiding riches are what we have stored in heaven.

DAY 7
a) Her sins (v. 14).
b) The coming destruction would cause despair; hope would arise as total destruction is ruled out and some would be saved (v. 12).

GUIDE TO STUDY 4

DAY 1   a) By living to gratify their own desires they were ruining the 'pasture' for others.
b) Oppression of the poor (did they influence their husbands to impose heavier taxes?) and drunkenness.
c) Personal; think of the influence they can have in the home.

DAY 2   He initiated an alternative system of worship with its shrines, festivals and priests to discourage the people from going to Jerusalem.

DAY 3   a) Their generosity in bringing their sacrifices and tithes.
b) They were boasting of what they had done; it was done for show.

DAY 4   a) Despite all his chastening through various disasters, the people had still not returned to Him.
b) As a Father disciplining them in love.

DAY 5   a) To prepare to meet God.
b) Because of their rejection of Him, God was indicating that He was going to take decisive action against the nation.

DAY 6   a) The coming again of the Lord Jesus and the day of judgment that will follow.
b) Through believing in the Lord Jesus.
Jesus may come at any moment.

DAY 7   a) To show them that God was in control of everything and able to carry out His threats against them.
b) Personal.

GUIDE TO STUDY 5

DAY 1
a) Amos is speaking as if Israel has already been overthrown.
b) She was weakened through corruption; the pagan nations wouldn't stand by her when the 'chips were down'.

DAY 2
a) Between life and death, between God and their current religious practices.
b) No-one but themselves; they had been warned.

DAY 3
a) Those who were poor and righteous.
b) They were very sinful.

DAY 4
a) They had been thinking that God was 'with' them (v. 14).
b) Abundant and eternal life.

DAY 5
a) God passing through a nation in judgment; great sorrow as a consequence.
b) That of having to endure the suffering of hell.

DAY 6
a) That the Day of the Lord would bring relief from their troubles. In fact, because of their sin, their troubles would increase.
b) The inevitability of divine judgment if we reject God's offer of salvation.

DAY 7
a) They were unacceptable.
b) Obedience is better than sacrifice.
c) They may seem attractive but will lead to eternal death. God has given us His Word to show us what He expects from us.

GUIDE TO STUDY 6

DAY 1 a) Their military conquests and material wealth.
b) No. In what God had done for them.

DAY 2 a) In a lavish, self-indulgent lifestyle.
b) The ruin of their country (v. 6).
c) A true faith will result in a practical concern for others.

DAY 3 a) Many could be cited. Psalm 63 illustrates his hunger and thirst for God.
b) Personal. It certainly will not help if we are disobeying God on some issue.

DAY 4 a) Divine hatred, conquest, death, the destruction of their material possessions.
b) God invokes Himself as the author of these things.

DAY 5 The breakdown of law and order; dishonouring marriage vows; the breakdown of family life, etc.

DAY 6 a) In a reversal of roles, Israel is now suffering defeat at the hands of another nation instead of being victorious.
b) God's way, as all other ways lead to death.

DAY 7 a) To bless them and make them a blessing to others.
b) No. No.
c) Yes.

GUIDE TO STUDY 7

DAY I
a) He realised that if God continued with this punishment the nation would not survive.
b) God responded to Amos's intercession.

DAY 2
a) A fire or drought consuming the crops – a picture of Israel's destruction.
b) He asked God to stop what He was doing, reminding Him of the nation's inability to survive it.

DAY 3
a) Concern and compassion
b) Intercede on their behalf.
c) That we seek God on behalf of others.

DAY 4
a) That it is not arbitrary but according to a well-defined standard.
b) Personal; perhaps like the Pharisee we have too high an opinion of ourselves. He missed out on God's righteousness.

DAY 5
a) That he was in the game of preaching for personal gain; that he was inciting rebellion against the king.
b) Personal; perhaps the sermon is too long, the people unfriendly, etc.

DAY 6
a) He was convinced that God had called him to this task.
His family would be ruined and he himself would be exiled to die in a pagan country.
b) Of being accepted by Christ when we come to Him; the Gospel is from God; God answers prayer.

DAY 7
His family would be ruined.

GUIDE TO STUDY 8

DAY 1 a) God was saying 'Time is up. The end has come. Your day of reckoning is here.'
b) People must have been desperately seeking deliverance.
c) God's reticence to judge provides opportunities for salvation. Sadly many (as in Noah's day) are not careful to use these opportunities to repent.

DAY 2 a) Incorrect weight given; balances rigged; sold chaff with the wheat.
b) They held back from trading on the Sabbath and on Festival Days (albeit reluctantly).

DAY 3 a) His ability to remember everything done.
b) To the Nile overflowing its banks.

DAY 4 a) Like mourning for an only child.
b) Mourning with and without hope. Christians have hope beyond the grave.

DAY 5 a) Wanting to hear from God and not being able to do so.
b) It purifies, gives direction and understanding, it saves.
Personal. We should value it while we have the privilege of having it.

DAY 6 a) The younger generation.
b) They were, at heart, idol worshippers.

DAY 7 Both suffered a dramatic change in fortune: from having plenty to having nothing; from a life of ease to one of suffering. Both could not reverse the change in their situations. Lack of obedience to God's Word is implied for the rich man's situation (Luke 16:31); Israel had committed the same sin.

GUIDE TO STUDY 9

DAY 1 a) Sin was dealt with at the altar; sacrifices were offered to God for the atonement of sin.
b) The temple would be destroyed.
During this earthquake.

DAY 2 a) As being frantic; every possible avenue of escape is explored.
b) The people could never get beyond the reach of God; He had determined that none would escape.

DAY 3 a) Both are references to people trying to escape God's judgment.
b) To hide from God.

DAY 4 a) Just one touch of God.
b) We should fear Him.

DAY 5 a) He reminds them (in their sinful state) that they were no better than any other nation.
b) That because they were Jews their nation would not suffer.

DAY 6 a) As being sinful.
b) The wicked are destroyed and the righteous preserved.

DAY 7 a) To something being carefully sieved (perhaps soil or grain).
b) Total destruction for the 'house of Jacob' is ruled out.
c) The sinners, those who mocked Amos' prophecy of disaster.

GUIDE TO STUDY 10

DAY 1 The NIV uses such words as 'broken places', 'ruins', 'exiled people', etc.

DAY 2 a) Their exile, suffering and poverty.
b) Death or sorrow.

DAY 3 a) Israel has been set up again as a nation; many Jews are returning to Israel.
b) The symbolic language used in verse 13.

DAY 4 a) Other nations.
b) The Lord Jesus.

DAY 5 a) To debate if Gentile converts were required to observe Jewish law, especially the issue of circumcision.
b) Verse 16.
c) The conversion of Gentiles is seen as fulfilling what Amos had prophesied even though at first glance Amos' words seem only to refer to Israel.

DAY 6 a) God can restore things as they used to be in spite of failure on our part.
b) If we acknowledge/confess our sins God will forgive us.

DAY 7 a) Amos' words. God.
b) He was inspired by the Holy Spirit.

THE WORD WORLDWIDE

We first heard of WORD WORLDWIDE over 20 years ago when Marie Dinnen, its founder, shared excitedly about the wonderful way ministry to one needy woman had exploded to touch many lives. It was great to see the Word of God being made central in the lives of thousands of men and women, then to witness the life-changing results of them applying the Word to their circumstances. Over the years the vision for WORD WORLDWIDE has not dimmed in the hearts of those who are involved in this ministry. God is still at work through His Word and in today's self-seeking society, the Word is even more relevant to those who desire true meaning and purpose in life. WORD WORLDWIDE is a ministry of WEC International, an interdenominational missionary society, whose sole purpose is to see Christ known, loved and worshipped by all, particularly those who have yet to hear of His wonderful name. This ministry is a vital part of our work and we warmly recommend the WORD WORLDWIDE 'Geared for Growth' Bible studies to you. We know that as you study His Word you will be enriched in your personal walk with Christ. It is our hope that as you are blessed through these studies, you will find opportunities to help others discover a personal relationship with Jesus. As a mission we would encourage you to work with us to make Christ known to the ends of the earth.

Stewart and Jean Moulds – British Directors, **WEC International**.

A full list of over 50 'Geared for Growth' studies can be obtained from:

ENGLAND   John and Ann Edwards
5 Louvain Terrace, Hetton-le-Hole, Tyne & Wear, DH5 9PP
Tel. 0191 5262803 Email: rhysjohn.edwards@virgin.net

IRELAND   Steffney Preston
33 Harcourts Hill, Portadown, Craigavon, N. Ireland, BT62 3RE
Tel. 028 3833 7844 Email: sa.preston@talk21.com

SCOTLAND Margaret Halliday
10 Douglas Drive, Newton Mearns, Glasgow, G77 6HR
Tel. 0141 639 8695 Email: m.halliday@ntlworld.com

WALES   William and Eirian Edwards
Penlan Uchaf, Carmarthen Road, Kidwelly, Carms., SA17 5AF
Tel. 01554 890423 Email: Penlan.uchaf@farming.co.uk

UK CO-ORDINATOR
Anne Jenkins
2 Windermere Road, Carnforth, Lancs., LA5 9AR
Tel. 01524 734797 Email: anne@jenkins.abelgratis.com

UK Website: www.wordworldwide.org.uk

Christian Focus Publications

publishes books for all ages

Our mission statement –

STAYING FAITHFUL

In dependence upon God we seek to help make His infallible word, the Bible, relevant. Our aim is to ensure that the Lord Jesus Christ is presented as the only hope to obtain forgiveness of sin, live a useful life and look forward to heaven with Him.

REACHING OUT

Christ's last command requires us to reach out to our world with His gospel. We seek to help fulfill that by publishing books that point people towards Jesus and help them to develop a Christ-like maturity. We aim to equip all levels of readers for life, work, ministry and mission.

Books in our adult range are published in three imprints.

Christian Focus contains popular works including biographies, commentaries, basic doctrine, and Christian living. Our children's books are also published in this imprint.

Mentor focuses on books written at a level suitable for Bible College and seminary students, pastors, and other serious readers. The imprint includes commentaries, doctrinal studies, examination of current issues, and church history.

Christian Heritage contains classic writings from the past.

For details of our titles visit us on our website
www.christianfocus.com

ISBN 0 908067 06 2

Copyright © WEC International

Published in 2002 by
Christian Focus Publications, Geanies House,
Fearn, Ross-shire, IV20 ITW, Scotland
and
WEC International, Bulstrode, Oxford Road,
Gerrards Cross, Bucks , SL9 8SZ

Cover design by Alister MacInnes

Printed and bound by J.W Arrowsmith, Bristol